Limits of Vulnerability

Exploring a Kenotic Model for Pastoral Ministry

Vanessa Herrick

Assistant Curate, St Edmundsbury Cathedral

GROVE BOOKS LIMITED
RIDLEY HALL RD CAMBRIDGE CB3 9HU

Contents

Acknowledgements

Many people have offered support and encouragement as I have explored this topic. Thanks are especially due to The Revd Dr Jeremy Begbie and the Revd Michael Roberts who supervised the MA dissertation which formed the basis for this booklet. I am also grateful to The Very Revd James Atwell, Provost of St Edmundsbury Cathedral, for allowing me time to write, and to my husband David, and sons Adam and Peter for their support, patience and encouragement. Lastly, my thanks to the Revd Ivan Mann, in whom I have recognized the vulnerability of Christ, and to whom this booklet is affectionately dedicated.

I am hoping to publish a fuller treatment of this subject under the title *Jesus Wept: Reflections on Vulnerability in Leadership* (DLT, late 1998).

The Cover Illustration is by Peter Ashton

First Impression September 1997
ISSN 0144-171X
ISBN 1 85174 353 7

1

Introduction

A friend of mine admitted, recently, to having broken down in the middle of preaching a funeral sermon. He had become especially close to the man who had died, had brought him to faith in Christ and supported him through a lengthy terminal illness. His parishioner's death had affected him deeply. But was he right to cry? Should he have been more 'professional'? How appropriate was it for him to allow *his* vulnerability to be seen?

'Vulnerable' is a fashionable word. The problem with fashionable words is that they become very hard to define. Their frequent use tends to mean that understanding is assumed and impact is lost. 'She's a vulnerable child'; 'It is a vulnerable situation'; 'The country has a vulnerable economy.'

What *does* it mean to be 'vulnerable,' and, more specifically, what does it mean for Christian leaders and pastors? *The Shorter Oxford English Dictionary* traces the roots of the word 'vulnerability' to the Latin *'vulnerabilis'* and the verb *'vulnerare'* meaning 'to wound.' Rarely, the verb is used in the *active* sense of 'having power to wound.' More commonly, it is used *passively* to describe 'that which may be wounded or susceptible of receiving wounds or physical injury.' It is also used figuratively to describe one who is 'open to attack or injury of a non-physical nature.'

An increasing number of Christian pastoral and spiritual writers have approached the idea of 'being vulnerable' as an integral feature of good pastoral practice. Stephen Pattison, in *A Critique of Pastoral Care* (London: SCM, 2nd ed, 1993) comments

> 'The basic notion...is that as by the wounds of Christ we have been healed, so it is the weaknesses, vulnerabilities, griefs and sorrows of the pastor which enable her to come close to others and minister to them' (p 151).

But to be vulnerable in this way is a matter of choice. It is to choose to open oneself to the possibility of being wounded; it is a 'removal of the mask,' a 'letting down of the defences.' Vulnerability, in the sense in which we are using it, involves a measure of control. For our purposes then, we shall define vulnerability as:

An openness to being wounded (physical or otherwise) which is the outcome of a voluntary relinquishment of the power to protect oneself from being wounded.

In his incarnation, God chose to make himself vulnerable in the person of Jesus Christ. He was not a victim. Rather, he chose to limit himself to the extent that he did not protect himself, but rather freed others to do their worst to him—

even if that meant death on a cross.

It may or may not have been appropriate for my friend to cry when preaching at a funeral. It may or may not have been 'professional.' It is worth remembering, however, that Jesus wept at the death of his friend Lazarus (John 11.35). He allowed who he was to be seen; and *his* vulnerability was not limited to tears at a funeral. *His* vulnerability was one which led ultimately to his death on the cross of Calvary. To the question of how God could become so vulnerable, we must now turn.

2

Jesus Christ Limited or Jesus Christ and Co? The Business of Kenotic Christology

The notion that 'in Jesus Christ, God limited himself in some aspect of his being or person to live a human life'[1] lies at the heart of what has come to be known as kenotic Christology. It has been defined as:

> 'a doctrine of the Incarnation which asserts some real modification of the divine attributes as a necessary condition of the true and personal entrance of the Son of God into human history' (Fairweather in Beare, *A Commentary on the Epistle to the Philippians* [London: A & C Black, 1959] p 159).

Its fundamental concern is the centuries-old Christological question concerning the divine status of the incarnate Son of God. It was of particular concern to the Fathers of the early church, and also during the Enlightenment period, when renewed interest in the *humanity* of the historical Jesus, together with the development of modern psychology, forced scholars of the period either to abandon any notion that Christ was divine, or to attempt to 'mould' traditional orthodoxy in such a way that Christ's divinity was upheld, but (more often than not) in some way *modified*, so as to allow his humanity to conform to newly-conceived understandings of the human person. Much metaphysical speculation ensued, especially concerning the retention, abstention from or modification of the divine attributes in the incarnate Son.

---

1   Dawe, D G, *The Form of a Servant. A Historical Analysis of the Kenotic Motif* (Philadelphia: Westminster Press, 1963).

It is of particular interest for our purposes, because it impinges on the question of whether and how the incarnate Son, in so limiting himself, chose to be vulnerable. In this chapter, therefore, we shall attempt to explore—briefly—the biblical roots of *kenosis* in Philippians 2 and then to address some of the critical issues which have arisen in respect of kenotic Christology. Thereafter, we shall endeavour to show that a relational rather than a metaphysical approach to the divinity of the incarnate Son is a more fruitful one, especially in respect of kenosis and vulnerability.

Biblical Roots of kenosis

The term kenosis comes from the Greek *kenoo*, meaning literally 'to empty, to make empty,' or inferentially 'to make of no effect.' It finds its scriptural *locus classicus* in Philippians 2.7—'but he emptied [*ekenosen*] himself taking the form of a slave,' where Paul (either himself, or in the words of traditional Christian hymnody) exhorts his readers to model their corporate life on the 'mind' or 'attitude' of Christ Jesus. The example of Christ (vv 5-11) is presented in the context of a passage about practical living (2.1-4 and 12ff). Indeed, Paul's intention would appear to be primarily to teach and encourage the Philippian Christians to follow Christ's example in daily living, rather than to write an essay in Christology! Nevertheless it is key for any discussion of kenosis.

Four interrelated phrases must be examined.[2] Firstly, in v6: *en morphe Theou*—'in the form of God.' The traditional, anti-Arian exegesis of this phrase suggested that 'in the form of God' did not mean mere likeness or similarity but rather that the incarnate Son was fully equal and co-eternal with the Father. This phrase is thus important, because some commentators make a direct connection between it and the phrase 'but he emptied himself' of v7, suggesting that it was, in some way, this 'form of God' of which Christ emptied himself. The kenoticists, in particular, objected to the Patristic (Victorinus and Athanasius) interpretation of the phrase, preferring to see 'in the form of God' as referring to those attributes of divinity which the Son renounced when he became human such as his pre-existent nature (Gore) or his equality with God, in terms of glory and divine prerogatives (Lightfoot). Karl Barth, however, saw it differently. For him, Christ's self-emptying was, paradoxically, a *'taking on'*—a choosing to 'take the form of a slave'(Phil 2.7), in addition to his divine form, in order to live a fully human life. Jesus was no less God.[3] Rather, the divine encompassed the

---

2   Here I am particularly indebted to N T Wright's chapter 'Jesus Christ is Lord' in *The Climax of the Covenant* (Edinburgh: T & T Clark, 1991).

3   Barth is insistent that if the incarnate Son, as Jesus, ceases—in any way—to be the eternal Son of God, then this has enormous implications for our understanding of salvation: 'We cannot possibly understand or estimate [the Christological mystery] if we try to explain it by a self-limitation or de-divinisation of God in the unity of the Son of God with the man Jesus. If in Christ—even in the humiliated Christ born in a manger at Bethlehem, and crucified on the cross of Golgotha—God is not unchanged and wholly God, then everything that we may say about the reconciliation of the world made by God in this humiliated One is left hanging in the air' (CD iv, 1, p 183).

human without stifling it or swallowing it up.

Tom Wright also explores at great length the use of the Greek word *harpagmos*, meaning variously, 'a thing to be plundered/clung on to/grasped or snatched,' and its link to its object, 'equality with God.' Debate has focused on two questions. Firstly, in what does this equality consist—divinity itself (kenotic view), divine prerogatives (Lightfoot), or divine equality (Latin Fathers, Barth, Moule, Hoover)? Secondly, is this equality the incarnate Son's *'by right'* (and therefore did not need to be snatched), or is it an equality he *already possessed* (and therefore did not need to be clung on to). Wright convincingly combines Hoover's philology and Moule's theology, suggesting that what is important is not whether or not (or how or when) equality is possessed, (for Wright believes, rightly, that the incarnate Son never ceased to be God), but rather what matters is 'the attitude one will take towards something one already has and holds and will continue to have and hold' (1991, p 78). He thus sees Christ's attitude to his equality with God as one of 'not taking advantage.' The thrust of Philippians 2.5-11 then, is that God, in the incarnate Son, chose to limit himself. The self-emptying of the Son of God was thus about self-negation, about making himself powerless and becoming vulnerable, not because he had to, but because he chose to. He did not negate his divinity, but rather fulfilled it, because that was the most appropriate way for him to express his divine equality in the human context.

The Development of Kenotic Christology

Over the course of history, the expression of the kenotic motif has varied according to the prevalent thought-world. For example, when the early church struggled with the question of Christ's self-emptying, it was in the context of a world where the thinking of the Greeks (especially Plato) was particularly influential. To the Greek mind, it was inconceivable for the eternal and divine to inhabit the changing and decaying environment of mortals. It is not surprising, therefore, that the Fathers of the church struggled over several centuries, (and with several swings of the pendulum), to reconcile the divinity and humanity of the incarnate Son of God (for example at the Councils of Nicea, 325CE, Constantinople, 381CE, and Chalcedon, 451CE). Their final (if not entirely adequate) solution was to ascribe to the incarnate Son *'two natures in one person, without confusion, without change, without division, without separation'* (Chalcedon, 451CE). Such an ascription sounds strange to us because our understanding of person has been informed by the developments of psychology over the past 150 years. We tend to think of 'person' in terms of 'personality,' that is, in a limited way. When Chalcedon spoke of the 'person' of the incarnate Son, it would have been understood to encompass body, soul, will and centre of consciousness. Thus, for Chalcedon, the 'person' of the incarnate Son means the eternal Son of God who assumed a full and complete human nature. It was not a case of 'either...or,' but of 'both...and.'

By the nineteenth century, the question of Christ's self-emptying was becoming particularly pertinent, as theologians (especially in Germany and England) tried to reconcile their new-found interest in the historical Jesus with their new-found insights into human psychology. A wide variety of suggestions were made as to how the incarnate Son could be fully human and fully divine, ranging from complete abandonment of divinity to partial renunciation or 'veiling' of some or all of the Son's divine attributes. The trap into which the kenoticists had fallen, however, was to look at the questions of Christ's self-emptying in a purely metaphysical way.

A 'Relational' Approach: The Role of the Holy Spirit

John Owen, the Puritan Divine, had seen the potential of a relational Christology back in the seventeenth century. Alan Spence, in his article 'Christ's Humanity and Ours: John Owen',[4] presents Owen's understanding that Jesus was to be regarded as 'the prototype of Christian existence, and as continually empowered, comforted and sanctified by the Holy Spirit' (p 75). Owen's view is that 'the eternal Son assumed human nature into personal union with himself, but…all direct divine activity on that assumed nature was that of the Holy Spirit' (pp 75-6). The *eternal Son* was in relationship with the Father and the Spirit by virtue of his divinity, and the *incarnate Son* was in relationship with the Father, *through* the Spirit in his humanity.

The incarnate Son thus both related God to humanity and humanity to God as a 'priest…beset with weakness' (p 87) (cf Heb 4.15 and 5.7), who knew, in his humanity, the 'spiritual desertion and separation from all comfort and joy in his relation with God the Father, and which culminated in his cry of dereliction from the cross' (p 87). For Owen, the possibility that the incarnate Son *experienced* this sense of desertion is not because he ceased to be divine, but because in his humanity, 'his experience of God is not immediate but indirect and by means of the Spirit' (p 88).

In addition, Spence sees Owen's presentation of the incarnate Son, acting in his human nature *only* as directed by the Holy Spirit, as an enormously encouraging example for humanity,. For it is the same Spirit, through whom the Father relates to the Son and the Son relates to the Father, who is the Spirit through whom the Father relates *through the Son* to humanity and humanity relates *through the Son* to the Father.

Owen clearly saw the incarnate Son in relation both to humanity and to the Trinity. It is remarkable that such a relational understanding should have been almost entirely absent during the nineteenth and early twentieth centuries, when kenotic Christology was at its height (caused in part, no doubt, by the fact that pneumatology was also at the 'low ebb'). Rather than perceiving the incarnate

4   In Schwöbel, C and Gunton, C E, *Persons, Divine and Human* (Edinburgh: T & T Clark, 1991).

Son in relational terms, his divinity and humanity were approached in a rational, metaphysical way, bringing about the intractable problems of Christology which we have attempted to clarify above.

Schwöbel, in his introductory chapter to *Trinitarian Theology Today: Essays on Divine Being and Act* (Edinburgh: T & T Clark, 1995), seeks to overcome this crisis in modern theology by offering an alternative 'trinitarian hermeneutic for Christology' in which he sees the worshipping Christian community, in relationship already with the triune God, as the starting point for Christological reflection. Such a hermeneutic moves from considering 'natures' to 'persons'— that is, it sees the incarnate Son not as *possessing a divine nature*, but rather in terms of the Son's relationship to the Father, through the Spirit. Personal distinction and personal communion of the Godhead is thus maintained, but as with John Owen, the Spirit's role in relation to the incarnate Son is vital. According to Schwöbel, 'trinitarian Christology is always pneumatological Christology and *vice versa*' (p 141).

One of the outcomes of the trinitarian hermeneutic is that it is no longer necessary to think of the incarnate Son *only* in terms of one person with two natures (as per Chalcedon), but also (or instead!) as one person *in a double set of relationships*—with God and with humanity—through whom humanity is reconciled and brought back into relationship with the triune God.

The trinitarian hermeneutic also offers useful insights concerning Christ's entry into the limitations of time and space:

'The relationship between the Father, the Son and the Spirit is eternal, even though the incarnate Son relates to the Father in the Spirit in the created temporality of human life. Conversely, Christ relates as the Son to the Father in the Spirit in the incarnation in the temporal reality of human life, and this is not denied in asserting that this relationship is eternally the relationship of the Son to the Father in the Spirit' (Schwöbel, *ibid*, p 143).

A 'receptacle' view of time and space is thus inappropriate: only a relational model will suffice. In the incarnate Son, God *chooses* to relate to humanity within the bounds of space and time, because that is the only appropriate and faithful way in which he can relate to them:

'Jesus is God's love taking place in our time and history' (Gunton in *Yesterday and Today: A Study of Continuities in Christology*, London: DLT, 1983, p 125).

It is not simply a matter of God in some way 'reducing' himself or 'squeezing' himself into human space and time. Rather, he took space and time into himself and created the 'place' of meeting, *par excellence*, in the person of the incarnate Son. Here, God meets people and people meet God. *Jesus* is the place in space and time where

'the vertical and the horizontal dimensionalities intersect, the place where human being is opened out to a transcendent ground in God and where the infinite Being of God penetrates into our existence and creates room for Himself within the horizontal dimension of finite being in space and time' (T F Torrance in *Space, Time and Incarnation*, Oxford: OUP, 1969, p 75).

It was the security of the incarnate Son's 'vertical' and 'horizontal' relationships which freed him to choose to be vulnerable to those around him. In his self-emptying, he limited himself in the sense that he did not take advantage of his divinity. That he was able to do so, and so relate appropriately in his humanity to those around him, within the bounds of space and time, was because of the trinitarian community of love in which he continued to dwell and of whose love for humanity he obediently became the vulnerable expression.

3

The Vulnerability of Jesus Christ:
Critical Moments in Luke's Gospel

In his gospel, Luke vividly presents the contrast between the *power* of God, seen, for example, in the often extraordinary miracles of healing, and the *powerlessness* of God, seen in his human weakness and vulnerability (for example, 9.58).[5]

His *power* is manifest in the form of 'mighty works' (4.36; 5.17; Acts 10.38), and authoritative words, spoken in the power of the Holy Spirit, both for healing (8.54), and for mission (9.3f). His *powerlessness*—or, to put it paradoxically— *the power of his powerlessness*, becomes evident through the way in which he sometimes placed himself in a vulnerable position in relation to both the religious and civil authorities (5.17, 21, 29-32; 6.6f; 11.53), and also his own family and community (4.16, 28ff; 8.19f). He knew what it was to take risks with people's expectations (5.4; 7.36f). He faced the consequences of speaking out (4.23f), and of remaining silent (23.9). He spoke of a way of life characterized by poverty, suffering and pain (6.20f); he taught in parables which illustrated the same (10.25f; 15.11f), and pointed to a child as an example of greatness (9.46-48). He emphasized the true cost of following his way (9.23; 14.27) and the demands of mission (9.3; 10.3 cf 12.11), and witnessed both by his teaching and his example to the truth that 'all who exalt themselves will be humbled, and those who humble themselves will be exalted' (14.11; 18.14; cf 22.26-27).

Yet it is in the 'key moments' of Jesus' life and ministry that his greatness and vulnerability are thrown into sharpest relief—in his birth, his baptism and temptations, his transfiguration and his passion. At these 'turning points,' we can recognize his dependence both on his *Father*, through the Holy Spirit, (often made explicit in the context of prayer), and also on his *closest and most intimate circle of disciples.*

Birth (Luke 1 and 2)

Luke's narrative of Jesus' birth combines the wonder and enormity of this event of cosmic significance, with the down-to-earth reality of the circumstances into which he was born. Both the social and physical contexts of Jesus' birth express a vulnerability, poverty and *insignificance* at odds with the angels' words of acclamation (1.26f; 2.6-7 cf 1.31-33; 2.11). Here is no special protection or immunity. Here God is enfleshed in the weakness of a vulnerable child.

Little is said of Jesus' childhood or his relationship with his earthly family at

---

5 This contrast is illustrated sharply in the story of the stilling of the storm, in which Jesus is subject *to* the storm, but also demonstrates his supreme authority *over* it (see 8.22ff).

this time (but see 2.40; 2.51-52). The prominence given by Luke to the role of the Holy Spirit in the events surrounding Jesus' birth, however, at the Annunciation (1.35), the Visitation (1.41f) and the Presentation (2.22f), establishes (implicitly) the child's relationship with his heavenly Father. The tension between the two sets of relationships is, perhaps, especially poignant in 2.41-51 when, (significantly, in the first words he utters in Luke's gospel), he indicates that whilst continuing for the time being to live in obedience to his earthly family (2.51), his *primary* relationship is with his heavenly Father. As the gospel unfolds, we see, increasingly, Jesus' dependence on his heavenly Father, and a shift in the focus of his *human* relationships from dependence upon his earthly family to dependence on his close followers (8.19-21).

Baptism and Temptation (3.21-4.13)

In his baptism (and again in the context of prayer) the human Jesus 'receives' the Holy Spirit and is affirmed in his identity as the eternal Son (3.21-22)—a relationship which will be questioned, almost immediately, by the devil in his repeated taunts, '*If* you are the Son of God…' (4.3,9). Indeed, we must not underestimate the significance of Jesus' temptations. For it is the Spirit who *leads* Jesus into the wilderness, the place of temptation. Jesus is not 'cushioned' from evil, but rather placed in a vulnerable situation—both physically (in terms of place, cf 9.58, and state, 4.2b), and spiritually (4.2a), and yet given both the strength and grace to endure it.

The Transfiguration (9.18-36)

During the early part of Jesus' teaching ministry, Luke emphasizes the 'great crowds' who flock to listen to him (4.42; 5.1; 6.17). As the gospel proceeds, however, Jesus' teaching becomes more focused towards what might be described as *circles of intimacy*. These range from the comparative anonymity of the great crowds, through his disciples, to the seventy-two (10.1), to the twelve apostles (6.12-16; 9.1), and finally to the three—Peter, James and John (8.51; 9.28; 22.8). The teaching and insight granted to each group varies (8.9-10; 10.22-24), as does the extent to which Jesus reveals his own feelings and needs (12.49-50; 22.14-15, 39f).

This principle of *circles of intimacy* and *degrees of disclosure* becomes very evident in Luke's account of the Transfiguration. For here, at this turning point in his ministry, we see again the importance of Jesus' relationships, both with his Father and with his closest disciples. Just over a week earlier, he had spoken openly, for the first time, of his impending passion and death (9.21-22). He had sought reassurance from his disciples concerning his identity—from the point of view of the crowds (9.18-20), and now, (with echoes of his baptism, and *yet again* in the context of prayer), he receives that reassurance from his heavenly Father, in the presence of the intimate circle of Peter, James and John (9.28).

Passion (19.11-24.53)

A lack of understanding is the characteristic response to each of the Lukan predictions of Christ's suffering and death (9.21-22, 44-45; 17.25; 18.31-35). From the point at which Jesus 'set his face to go to Jerusalem' (9.51), we see him becoming increasingly vulnerable to the anger, misunderstanding and conspiracy of those against him (20.19; 22.2ff). Whilst continuing to teach, he becomes more and more passive in his attitude towards his opposers (22.53), recognizing that through *their* actions against him, his Father's will would be fulfilled. This passivity, and the openness to vulnerability which accompanies it, is borne out through Luke's use of the verb *paradidomi*, meaning 'to give, hand over to another.' Although occasionally used in respect of a 'thing' or 'commodity' (for example, 'authority' in 4.6), or in the sense of handing down a *tradition* (1.2, cf Acts 6.14; 16.4), it is most commonly used in Luke's gospel to indicate a *person* being handed over to another. It is a term used both *by* Jesus (12.58; 21.16), and *in respect of* Jesus (9.44; 18.32; 20.20; 23.25; 24.7,20; see also Acts 3.13).[6] Jesus becomes—by his own initiative—one who is *done to* and who exposes himself to risk. He allows himself to be vulnerable to what others will do to him, even though that may be infinitely costly, painful and destructive to himself.

Secure in his relationship with his heavenly Father, through the Holy Spirit, the incarnate Son of God opened himself up to the possibility of being wounded. Such a *chosen* vulnerability was an intrinsic aspect of his ministry, as Luke describes it, seen in his exercise of power, his experience of powerlessness, his rootedness in prayer and his willingness to free others to do their worst to him, because such was the way of obedience and the way of love. Yet this chosen vulnerability, this *kenosis* for the renewal of humanity, was intrinsic to his earthly ministry, supremely because it is intrinsic to who God is as Trinity, and to his relationship of love to all that he has created. Love is, and cannot but be, vulnerable, and the God who is Father, Son and Spirit, *is* Love.

---

6 W H Vanstone, in chapter 3 of *The Stature of Waiting* (London: DLT, 1982), presents a study of the verb *paradidomi* in the Gospels of Mark and John, and reaches a conclusion, which, we would suggest, may apply equally to the Gospel of Luke:

'What happens in both Mark and John when Jesus is handed over is not that He passes from success to failure, from gain to loss or from pleasure to pain: it is that He passes from doing to receiving what others do, from working to waiting, from the role of subject to that of object and, in the proper sense of the phrase, from action to passion' (1982, p 31).

4
A Kenotic Model Offered

It is tempting to look at the life and practice of Jesus Christ in his particular context two thousand years ago, and assume that our way of living and our pastoral practice must be identical. To do so is not only to fall into the trap of arrogantly presuming that we could in some way 'match up to' Jesus Christ, but it is also to ignore the dynamic of the Holy Spirit who enables us to live and engage appropriately with others in our own particular time and context, just as he enabled the incarnate Son to do so in his. 'Lifting' what Jesus said and did in a naïve way, and saying and doing the same may not always be appropriate!

Nevertheless, Scripture and tradition invite us to be 'imitators of Christ' (for example 1 Cor 11.1; 1 Thess 1.6), and shepherds modelled after the Good Shepherd (John 10 and the Ordinal). It is right, therefore, that we should look to Christ (and for our particular purposes, to the self-emptying and vulnerable Christ), to provide us with a model for living and a model for good pastoral practice which *may* include making space for vulnerability within the pastoral relationship.

Any principles which we elicit must be prefaced by the acknowledgement that of ourselves we cannot model ourselves on Jesus Christ.[7] We cannot 'imitate Christ' in the sense of copying him; we can only 'be imitators of Christ' in a dynamic way as, in Christ, by the Holy Spirit, and in obedience to the Father, we offer ourselves continually as channels of the love and grace of God. Indeed, it is only as, by the Holy Spirit, we are enabled to share in the ongoing priesthood of Christ, that we participate, as it were, in his ongoing vulnerability.

Five principles may be noted.

1. In a kenotic model for pastoral ministry, relationship is the basis for vulnerability.

It was, above all, the security of the incarnate Son's relationship with his heavenly Father, mediated in his humanity by the Holy Spirit, which freed him to be vulnerable to those around him—a relationship and identity affirmed, often in the context of prayer, both by his Father (Lk 3.22; 9.35) and by his followers (Lk 9.20). In his relationships with those around him, he risked varying degrees of disclosure amongst different circles of intimacy.

In pastoral ministry, it is the security of our relationship with God, mediated

---

7   The great challenge for Christians is to...learn how to de-egotize leadership, to find a model of kenotic leadership which leads for the sake of truth, for the sake of love, and not for any more complicated inner motive to do with the satisfactions of the exercise of power itself' (Richard Holloway, *The Divine Risk*, London: DLT, 1990, xvi).

by the same Holy Spirit, and strengthened and deepened by a life of prayer, which frees us to be vulnerable to those around us. The security and constraints of our *human* relationships (for example, our family, our community of faith) enhance our freedom to be vulnerable to others, with whom we too may risk varying degrees of disclosure amongst different circles of intimacy.

2. In a kenotic model for pastoral ministry, the Holy Spirit enables appropriate vulnerability.

The incarnate Son did not relate to all who came to him for help or teaching in exactly the same way. There was a variety of response, according to the other person's need. Particularity mattered. From time to time, it is clear that the faithful and appropriate way of relating made Jesus vulnerable to those around him (for example, the Sabbath healings, and Jesus' anointing by the 'sinful woman', Lk 7.36ff). The Holy Spirit generated an appropriate vulnerability according to a particular situation.

In pastoral ministry, we shall not relate to all who come to us in the same way. The work of the Holy Spirit is to enable faithful and appropriate ways of relating which enhance the particularity of those whom we serve. Being vulnerable to another may not always be appropriate; sometimes, the most 'caring' approach may be to retain a 'critical distance.' Nevertheless, there needs to be a *preparedness* to be vulnerable should the Holy Spirit prompt us in that way.

3. In a kenotic model for pastoral ministry, vulnerability leads to pain, suffering and growth.

Love always brings with it the risk of rejected love. The love of God for humanity, expressed in both redemption and creation, carried that risk. In his life, passion and death, the incarnate Son of God entered fully into the pain of suffering humanity, redeemed it through his cross and resurrection and carried it, in his exaltation, into the life of the Godhead.

In pastoral ministry, which is motivated by love, and which seeks to enable growth and renewal into the likeness of Christ, those who pastor can expect to be affected by those for whom they care. To enter into a pastoral relationship is to risk rejection, pain and suffering, for love demands an involvement with the other which, although it may be a 'key' to growth, may lead also to both suffering *with* them, and to suffering *because of* them. For vulnerability opens up a potentially limitless exchange of hurt as well as of love.

4. In a kenotic model for pastoral ministry, vulnerability may take the form of restraint or 'passive activity.'

The kenosis of the Son of God entailed restraint on his part, and a choosing to enter into the limitation and finitude of being human. Even within the bounds of space and time which that self-limitation brought, there were occasions when the incarnate Son chose to be silent in the face of false accusations, and to surrender himself to others in a form of 'passive activity'—that is, the active choice to do or say nothing—so freeing them to do their worst to him. In such apparent powerlessness and vulnerability, he risked both misunderstanding and accusations of utter weakness.

In pastoral ministry, we too are called to enter into relationships which are 'bounded' in terms of space, time and confidentiality. We need to beware the ever-present danger of smothering the other, and be continually concerned to preserve the particularity of both pastor and pastored. Within these bounds, it may or may not be appropriate to speak of our own experience and needs. Sometimes, vulnerability will take the form of actively going out towards the other and risking hurt or rejection. At other times, it may be more appropriate to be vulnerable by remaining silent, absorbing accusations and misunderstanding, rather than becoming defensive. As Rowan Williams has perceptively observed:

> 'To say something or to be silent with another person is to be out of cover' (in *The Divine Risk*, Richard Holloway (ed), London: DLT, 1990, p 12).

5. In a kenotic model for pastoral ministry, to be vulnerable is a matter of choice.

Jesus was not a victim of circumstance. He chose to empty himself and make himself vulnerable, both in his ministry of teaching and healing and supremely in his passion and death.

To be vulnerable is not the same as to be a victim. Unlike Christ, we are already finite and vulnerable by virtue of being human, yet we are still free to make choices within that network of constraint. We can still *choose* whether and with whom we share our own weaknesses and failures, even when the Holy Spirit may be clearly prompting us to do so!

5
A Kenotic Model Applied to Pastoral Ministry

Our explorations of a kenotic model for pastoral ministry make it clear that, although we can never imitate the totality and manner of Christ's self-emptying, nevertheless we find in him a pattern of ministry which is vulnerable, and which (as we have previously suggested) displays:

> *An openness to being wounded (physical or otherwise) which is the outcome of a voluntary relinquishment of the power to protect oneself from being wounded.*

Enabled by the Holy Spirit, from within the security of his relationship with his heavenly Father, the incarnate Son chose a path of obedience which led to misunderstanding, suffering and eventual death, and which, on his way, made him physically, spiritually and emotionally vulnerable to those around him.

The purpose of this chapter is to explore the place of vulnerability in pastoral relationships. Using as a framework, the five principles for a kenotic model for pastoral ministry, we will examine questions of boundaries and particularity, and also consider the costs, dangers and benefits of vulnerability both for those pastoring and being pastored. We will address the question of the relationship between vulnerability and professional ministry. Finally, we will consider vulnerability as a 'spiritual gift' and endeavour to establish a link between vulnerability and Christian hope.

1. Relationship as a Basis for Vulnerability

In chapter 2, we emphasized the importance of understanding the incarnate Son of God as one person 'in a double set of relationships—with God and with humanity—through whom humanity is reconciled and brought back into relationship with the triune God' (see p 8 above). That he existed, in his humanity, in that double set of relationships brought with it limitations and constraints. In his self-limitation, the incarnate Son of God operated within the bounds of space and time in such a way as to be faithfully and appropriately related to humanity. He was fully human and therefore shared in the limitations of being human. Yet he remained fully the eternal Son, and so continued to exist within the positive network of constraint which is the Trinity. The positive constraints of love which characterize the Godhead—constraints which (paradoxically) speak not of a 'holding in' but of an 'opening outwards'—enabled the incarnate Son, even in his humanity, to live in loving obedience to the Father, to receive the Father's affirmation, and the Spirit's anointing. The freedom and security which he knew in his relationships within the Trinity enabled him to move into the constraints and vulnerability of being human, for the sake of humanity.

As pastors, we too operate within particular boundaries and live within networks of constraint. For the act of 'entering into another's space' always raises the question (consciously or not) of how to relate. The establishment and maintenance of boundaries has been a matter of perennial importance in pastoral practice, be they spatial, temporal, physical or concerning information or knowledge.

At a first glance, the concept of boundaries may appear to be limiting in a negative way. Boundaries are usually in place either to keep someone or something in, or to keep others out. In pastoral ministry, boundaries do set limits (even if they are not always adhered to); they are, nevertheless, limits which exist to create freedom to relate within those limits, rather than to prevent relating. Nevertheless, it is the constraints of the relationships within which we already exist, (for example, with our partners, family, close friends, and even ecclesiastical structures) which free us to risk appropriate vulnerability in pastoral situations for the sake of those to whom we minister. To put it baldly, my security in my relationship with my marriage-partner should free me to be appropriately intimate with others who need reassurance in a physical way. It is true that such vulnerability is open to distortion by sin: the temptation is always there for appropriate intimacy to become inappropriate.

Boundaries and constraints help to maintain what the caring professions might describe as a 'critical distance' in pastoral care. Much has been written during the past twenty years on the importance of this empathetic approach to pastoral relationships. There is much insight and value in such an approach. Nevertheless, it sits uncomfortably with the notion of God who in Christ became intimately involved with humanity and who through the Holy Spirit fruitfully identified with and ministered to humanity. He did not maintain a critical distance from humanity. Rather, he entered fully into the human condition with all its suffering and pain, identified with it, shared in it, and experienced it for himself. That he was able to do so depended not only on his relationship with his Father through the Spirit, made particularly evident, as we have seen in Luke's Gospel, at key moments in his ministry and through his continuing life of prayer, but also on his relationships with those around him. He knew (by the prompting of the Holy Spirit) when and with whom to share his own vulnerability and how it was appropriate to behave.

Those involved in pastoral care are also called to risk this 'deep involvement' with other people. Such involvement will require support (in the form of prayer, spiritual direction or supervision), just as secular counsellors rely on networks of supervision, but it will not avoid the pain which inevitably accompanies much pastoral work. Rather, it will 'Rejoice with those who rejoice, and weep with those who weep' (Rom 12.15). It will depend, especially, on the maintenance of a healthy relationship with God, founded on a life of prayer. For from such an undergirding of prayer will come the wisdom and discernment by which the pastor may recognize when and with whom it may be appropriate to be vulnerable.

2. The Holy Spirit Enables Appropriate Vulnerability

In his humanity, the incarnate Son relied on the prompting of the Holy Spirit to know how to behave and what to say or not say in any given situation. Although he became deeply involved with humanity, he neither 'smothered' people nor lost his own distinctiveness in relation to them. He allowed those to whom he ministered space to be and to do as they chose, treating each as an individual, created and loved by God. Here was no 'distant,' 'professional' approach to pastoral care, in which persons are treated as 'cases' and the 'general' effaces the 'particular.' Rather, the outflowing of the love of the triune God, incarnated in the Son and poured out on humanity by the Spirit, surrounded and sustained the one cared for without, at any time, overwhelming him.[8]

For some, that ministry will be to offer strength, reliability, nurture and support; for others, the Spirit may require a willingness to minister out of weakness and vulnerability, offering identification, companionship and a sharing in pain. For some, it will be appropriate for the minister to speak of his or her *own* vulnerability, which may become a 'key' which unlocks the pain and vulnerability of others. Occasionally, it may be appropriate for a Christian pastor's woundedness to be shared amongst the congregation or community of faith, although this always carries with it the risk of egotism—of the vulnerability itself becoming something to 'display' or 'parade.' What is more likely is that there will be an intimate circle of those who will allow the pastor to face up to her woundedness, and who will, in turn, love and support her in her pain. Such an intimate circle frees the pastor from what Henri Nouwen has described as 'spiritual schizophrenia' (in *In the Name of Jesus: Reflections on Christian Leadership*, London: DLT, 1989, p 50), that is, of being spiritually 'secure' in public, but floundering and aware of considerable weakness and failing in private. Just as there are circles of intimacy, so too there will be degrees of disclosure. What is appropriate to share with one individual or group, may not be appropriately shared more widely.

It is the Holy Spirit who enables pastors to balance the need for distance and intimacy, boundaries and openness, identification and companionship and particularity. As we have seen, Jesus' own ministry was rooted in his relationship with his Father, through the Spirit, and maintained by a life of prayer. It is clear from the gospels that he dealt with people according to each one's particular

---

8 'Professionalism' in pastoral ministry—particularly over the last twenty years—has tended to promote detachment, problem-centredness, dependency and individualism, whereas *true* pastoral care is 'involved,' *growth*-centred, mutually upbuilding and rooted in the community of faith. It is nevertheless true that 'professionalism' in Christian pastoral ministry has been beneficial in terms of developing counselling skills and deeper understanding of the psychological dimensions of caring.

needs. Led by the Spirit, he also moved between vulnerability and strength,[9] and as he did so, he attracted some people and alienated others. He impressed many with his authority and power, yet to others he appeared weak and degraded (cf Lk 7.39), eating with sinners and mixing in 'wrong' company. Through the Holy Spirit, Jesus retained his own particularity as the incarnate Son of God, a particularity which identified him both as a vulnerable leader and a powerful one. His willingness to be vulnerable—even amongst those closest to him— carried with it considerable costs and dangers. Such is also the case for vulnerable pastors today.

3. Vulnerability Leads to Pain, Suffering and Growth

The incarnate Son knew the pain of being human, redeemed it through the cross and resurrection and carried it in his exaltation into the life of the Godhead. As the eternal high priest, he continues to share in the pain of suffering humanity, and so shares also the vulnerability of those who, through the Spirit, participate in that priesthood and seek to be channels of the Father's endless love. For vulnerability opens up a potentially limitless exchange of hurt as well as of love.

For a pastor to be vulnerable is a costly business, not only for the pastor, but also for her family, congregation and the wider establishment of which she may be a representative. As we have suggested, vulnerability can both attract and alienate, bring pain as well as growth, misunderstanding as well as benefits and challenge to others.

Contrasting the approach of the Christian leader with that of other professionals, Moody (in *Eccentric Ministry. Pastoral Care and Leadership in the Parish*, London: DLT, 1992) comments:

'God has taken the risk of identifying his own honour with the fortunes of his people...Anyone who is put in the position of disclosing God's faithfulness in leadership is open to the same dimension of risk...[T]o come between God and his people as a leader is inevitably to accept the risk of incurring anger, misunderstanding and rejection' (p 23).

When that leadership role is coupled with any admission of failure or weakness, then it can be costly, not only to the one who makes himself vulnerable, but to his family as well. Whether they articulate it or not, clergy families in particular often feel abused by those to whom one member of that family ministers.

It is when a pastor's failure or vulnerability becomes a matter for the wider

---

9 Compare, for example, his vulnerability to the woman who anointed him (Lk 7.36-50) with his incisive criticism of Simon the Pharisee in the same incident.

congregation, wider community or even the general public, that most pain is felt. Whatever the 'scandal,' the role of the media in communicating (and perhaps 'enlarging') the significance of a person's failure, surely does much to inhibit openness and any admission of weakness, especially if that person is a 'senior' church leader. As a rule, the general public does *not* cope with failure in leaders, especially if they have some 'pastoral care' of others (for example, teachers and social workers as well as clergy). The fantasy exists that such people should be morally 'above reproach' and people feel let down when this is evidently not the case. The media is not sympathetic in such instances, with the result that vulnerability made known on this scale is, almost inevitably, unhelpful and destructive.

There are costs too for those who are being pastored. There may be a sense of disillusion and discomfort which can arise when one upon whom another is, in some way, dependent, reveals her own weakness. To be vulnerable can create risk for others who need to lean on the one whom they think is strong. Such a dependency, however, may reveal both an inappropriate reliance on a human being rather than on God,[10] and also suggests a limited understanding of 'strength.' For it does not allow for the strength in weakness (cf 2 Cor 12.9; Heb 11.34). For in a paradoxical way, a person has to be strong to be vulnerable, a truth exemplified most fully in Jesus' own passion and death.

The greatest danger for those being pastored by one who is willing to be vulnerable, however, concerns the abuse of power. For even vulnerability can be used as a means of abuse. It is possible for the pastor to 'smother' the one for whom she is caring with her own weaknesses, or else to coerce the other into revealing their own weaknesses and needs, whether they choose to or not. In addition, by its very nature, vulnerability tends to be expressed both physically and emotionally. Tears may be shed and touch may become important. Here again, the question of appropriate boundaries arises, for a pastor may be guilty (consciously or not) of seeking some form of sexual solace through her ministry, and so become guilty of abusing the one to whom she is ministering.

Jesus was never guilty of abusing those for whom he cared. His love for them was too great and too perfect for that to have been possible. Yet in him too can be seen the costs of vulnerability—both physical (whether threatened—Lk 4.28-30, or actual—Lk 22.63-65) and emotional. He experienced danger, tears, frustration and pain. He too knew what it was to be rejected (Lk 4.28-30; 23.18), misinterpreted and misunderstood (Lk 22.66-23.24), and his family (and indeed his closest friends), shared the pain of his vulnerability (Lk 2.35; Jn 19.25-27; 21.15-19). To be vulnerable—despite its benefits—brings with it both costs and dangers.

---

10 Although since God's love is very often mediated through other human beings, it is difficult to assume this!

4. Vulnerability in the Form of Restraint or Passive Activity

Our study of the incarnate Son's vulnerability in Luke's gospel revealed a 'shift' over the course of his ministry from one of 'prophetic activity' to what we have termed as 'passive activity'—that is, a willingness simply to be present with another in such a way as to free them to respond to love offered, whatever the consequences for the one offering that love. Led by the Holy Spirit and in obedience to the Father, the incarnate Son made himself vulnerable in his passion, by giving others 'space' to do their worst to him without resistance. Silent in the face of false accusations, he absorbed the anger, misunderstanding and hate of those around him.

The temptation in pastoral care is always to say something—to offer comforting words, help or advice. It can also be tempting, in the face of tragedy, to become defensive about a suggested path of action which has gone awry. Being there, alongside another in his pain, especially when that pain is expressed in the form of anger towards the pastor, is one of the most demanding aspects of the pastoral encounter. To remain silent and to wait, risking both misunderstanding and accusations of weakness and incompetence, demands a maturity and vulnerability which is rare.

5. Vulnerability as a Matter of Choice

Christ's choosing to become vulnerable in his humanity was, and continues to be, a gift to humanity. In any pastoral relationship where Christian love motivates and the Holy Spirit directs, there is a gift of grace, and that grace is mediated through the listening, speaking and caring love of those within that relationship. The ability to love and be loved is always a gift of the One who is love. In a pastoral relationship where one or both parties choose to share weakness, or to allow themselves to be 'delivered up,' such grace is especially evident.

The element of choice remains, but the opportunity to make that choice, to follow the vulnerable path, is in itself a gift. In the passages from Luke which we discussed earlier (birth, baptism and temptation, transfiguration and passion—especially Gethsemane), we see something of the struggle which the human Jesus underwent in choosing to accept the gift of vulnerability. He was not a victim of imposed suffering, over which he had no control. Rather, his human will was moulded by the Holy Spirit to the divine will, so that he could accept the gift of following the way of suffering. He went to his death willingly and obediently, trusting that God would vindicate him, yet his human trust must have been stretched to the limit. Even for the Son of God, there had to be an assent to descent (cf Phil 2.7).

To think of vulnerability as a 'gift' may, at first, seem odd. Why should a God of love offer a gift which seems so costly to the one who receives it? The answer lies, surely, in the mystery of all gifts of grace—that is, that they are always given to one for the sake of the other (cf 1 Cor 12.7). A gift of vulnerability, accepted and offered in the context of Christian love can be the means through which the Spirit opens others out to greater measures of that love. As with all of God's gifts, it will never be imposed, it can only be received. Gethsemane makes that clear.

In addition, a gift of vulnerability can always be a sign of hope. One of Jürgen Moltmann's greatest contributions to theology has been his understanding of 'Christianity as eschatology'—of God's promise 'breaking in from the future'—and his suggestion that the cross, resurrection and coming of the Spirit are not solely historical events of the past, but also anticipatory events of the coming kingdom, when there will be no more pain (Rev 21.4) (see his *Theology of Hope*, London: SCM, 1967). It is tempting to think that to focus on vulnerability is, in some way, to deny Christianity as eschatology, to deny the promise of the kingdom and even the efficacy of the cross. In pastoral ministry, it is easy to lose this dimension of hope in the midst of vulnerability and pain, either by denying the pain itself, or by becoming so immersed in it that there seems to be no future and no way out. Yet to admit to vulnerability in ourselves and others is to acknowledge the incompleteness of that promised future. It is to acknowledge the continued existence of sin and present suffering and pain, but it is to do so in the light of God's promises for the future. Scripture makes it clear that there is a time dimension to kenosis; there had to be descent before ascent in Philippians 2. And the Christ who spoke the words of Psalm 22 at his crucifixion, was the same Christ who 'for the sake of the joy that was set before him endured the cross, disregarding its shame, and has taken his seat at the right hand of the throne of God' (Heb 12.2). Like Christ and the prophets of the Old Testament before him, the pastor who is prepared to be vulnerable and willing to stay with his own and another's pain can be a sign of trust in the God of promise and the God of hope, for by his very presence he incarnates the presence of God, by the Holy Spirit—the presence of the God who in himself encompasses past, present and future.

In our discussion so far, we have considered the importance of boundaries in relating, the dangers, costs and benefits of vulnerability in the pastoral relationship, and vulnerability as a gift and a sign of hope. There is an element of risk and vulnerability in any pastoral relationship—including a 'professional' caring relationship—whether or not that vulnerability is acknowledged. To consciously make oneself vulnerable, to choose to 'empty oneself' of the power to protect oneself from being wounded by others, is to accept a gift which is costly, but which carries with it the promise of redemption through the one 'who, though he was in the form of God, did not regard equality with God as something to be exploited, but emptied himself...' (Phil 2.6-7f). A willingness to follow the leading of the Holy Spirit, to make that choice and to risk the outcome is the mark of the pastor whose security in relationship with God is fostered by a life of prayer, and whose security in relationship with those closest to him frees him to reveal both weakness and strength as the Spirit directs. Such a chosen vulnerability will neither be appropriate for every pastoral encounter, nor in every context. Yet when it *is* appropriate, and when risks are taken, then the love of God may flow more freely, and the people of God may grow more into the likeness of Jesus Christ.

6

The Challenge of Vulnerability

Our explorations of a kenotic model for pastoral ministry have pointed again and again to the example of the self-emptying Christ, who in his incarnation, passion and death demonstrated a willingness to make himself vulnerable. This is not to suggest that he exercised no power and had no authority. Nevertheless, he did not hide behind it. Rather, he allowed who he was to be seen—not by everybody and not at all times—but amongst varying circles of intimacy, with varying degrees of disclosure. He did not hide from those closest to him, and did not (and could not) hide from his heavenly Father. His vulnerability brought him pain, rejection and misunderstanding, and yet through the Holy Spirit, it also became the vehicle for the Father's love for humanity.

Those who exercise pastoral leadership in the church today sometimes struggle with the tension between who they are and the roles they perform. As 'religious professionals' they are expected not only to be competent managers and administrators and skilled 'technicians of the sanctuary,'[11] but also able pastoral counsellors. As 'professionals' they are expected to be properly trained, properly accountable and to operate with a suitable professional 'detachment' from their clients. They are to keep their personal agenda separate form their work agenda, and not allow their own responses and emotions to be seen by those with whom they work. In short, they are to be invulnerable.

Such a picture is, perhaps, a parody…but perhaps it is not. Those who exercise pastoral leadership *should* be professional about the way they work. Skills and techniques acquired in training are important and useful, be they theological, administrative, liturgical or pastoral. In the pastoral area especially, the psychological and other insights gained through counselling training can be

---

11 Anthony Russell in *The Clerical Profession* (London: SPCK, 1980).

immensely helpful in working with anxious and disturbed people, and a recognition of the appropriate place of boundaries and supervision in the pastoral relationship is vital for pastor and pastored alike.

Yet being professional and being professionally trained is not *all* there is to pastoral leadership. There is, surely, another dimension—one which the management and technique-oriented church of the late twentieth century is in danger of losing. It is that dimension which distinguishes Christian pastoral care from secular therapies. Only possible in the relational context of which we have spoken, it is founded on a life of prayer. It may bring pain, but it also brings growth, and its appropriateness must be discerned according to the promptings of the Holy Spirit. It is a dimension for which you cannot be 'trained' in the sense of acquiring skills—it is more a 'letting go.' It is the dimension which allows Christ to be seen through the vulnerability of the one who offers himself as a channel for the Father's love—not because of any skill or technique, valuable as those may be, but simply because he has chosen to risk 'removing the mask.' It is the dimension through which the vulnerability of the self-emptying Christ is incarnated in those who follow him today.